Leading with Vision:
A Guide to Hospital Service Line Leadership

Table of Contents

Introduction

Chapter 1: The Role of a Service Line Leader

Chapter 2: Building a Strategic Vision for Service Line Success

Chapter 3: Developing Collaborative Leadership

Chapter 4: Creating an Efficient Operational Structure

Chapter 5: Enhancing Patient Experience

Chapter 6: Managing Financial Performance

Chapter 7: Fostering Innovation and Continuous Improvement

Chapter 8: Navigating Regulatory and Compliance Challenges

Chapter 9: Leading Through Change

Chapter 10: Developing and Retaining Talent

Chapter 11: Ethical Leadership in Healthcare

Conclusion

Introduction: Welcome to Service Line Leadership

Welcome! If you're reading this, you're likely stepping into the exciting and challenging role of a service line leader—or preparing for it. First off, congratulations! It's a rewarding position with incredible opportunities to make a difference in both patient care and the overall functioning of your organization. But let's be honest—there will be challenges along the way. You'll be navigating the intersection of clinical care, operations, finances, and leadership, which can feel like a balancing act. The good news is, you don't have to go through it alone. This book is here to guide you through the complexities of service line leadership and help you thrive.

You might be feeling overwhelmed at the prospect of leading a service line. After all, you're now responsible for a diverse range of tasks—overseeing clinical outcomes, managing budgets, ensuring patient satisfaction, and aligning your team's work with the strategic goals of your hospital. It can feel like you're expected to be an expert in everything overnight. Take a breath—you don't have to know it all right away. Leadership is a journey, and the fact that you're here already shows you're committed to growing and learning. This book is designed to help you understand your role better, equipping you with practical strategies and insights to become an exceptional service line leader.

Why Leadership in Healthcare Matters

Let's start with the big picture—why does leadership in healthcare matter so much? In healthcare, the stakes are incredibly high. Every decision you make can impact not just the efficiency of your service line but also the lives of your patients. As a leader, you're not just managing tasks or teams. You're guiding your department through complexity, ensuring the well-being of your staff, and ultimately driving outcomes that directly affect patient care.

Your leadership also sets the tone for the entire department. Have you ever noticed how the culture of a team reflects its leadership? If you're transparent, supportive, and focused on a shared vision, your team will likely mirror those values. On the other hand, inconsistent or disconnected leadership can lead to a lack of direction, low morale, and even poor patient outcomes. This is why being intentional about your leadership style is crucial. You're shaping not just processes but the entire atmosphere in which patient care is delivered.

As a service line leader, you're also the crucial link between your team's day-to-day activities and the broader strategic goals of your hospital or health system. Whether the organization is focusing on value-based care, improving patient experience, or expanding market reach, your role is to ensure your service line contributes to those priorities. This is where your leadership can make a real, tangible difference.

What Is a Service Line, Anyway?

Let's take a step back for a moment and define what exactly a service line is. While the term can vary slightly depending on the hospital or health system, a service line typically refers to a group of related services that focus on a specific area of patient care—such as cardiology, oncology, neurology, or women's health.

As the leader of a service line, you're responsible for coordinating all the moving parts within that area. This includes not only clinical care but also operations, finances, and aligning with the hospital's strategic vision. Think of yourself as the CEO of your service line. You'll work closely with physicians, nurses, administrators, and various departments to ensure that everything runs smoothly and that your team is delivering high-quality care while meeting financial and operational goals.

Sound like a lot? It is. But it's also a fantastic opportunity to create real impact. When everything clicks—when your team is aligned, your outcomes are strong, and your service line is thriving—it's incredibly rewarding. You're not just a manager checking off boxes; you're a leader shaping the future of healthcare delivery in your organization.

Why This Book?

You might be wondering, why write a book about service line leadership? The answer is simple—I've been where you are now. When I first stepped into a service line leadership role, I found myself searching for practical guidance, something to help me understand how to balance clinical excellence with financial sustainability, and how to lead a diverse team through change. I wished there had been a roadmap, and that's why I wrote this book—to provide you with the guide I wish I had.

Over the years, I've gathered a wealth of knowledge, not only from my own experiences but also from other leaders in healthcare. This book pulls together those insights into a practical guide, offering you the tools and strategies you'll need to succeed. Whether it's about building a strategic vision, understanding hospital operations, managing a team, or balancing clinical care with financial performance, this book is here to help.

This book is for everyone—whether you're coming from a clinical background or an administrative one. One of the themes you'll see throughout is the importance of bridging the gap between clinical care and hospital operations. Both are essential to the success of your service line, and as a leader, it's your job to navigate both worlds effectively.

What to Expect

Here's what you can expect as we move through the book. We'll start with the basics—defining your service line's vision, aligning your goals with your hospital's strategic priorities, and understanding the financial landscape. These are the building blocks of effective leadership, and we'll spend time making sure you have a solid foundation.

Next, we'll move into the operational aspects of your role. How do you identify inefficiencies in hospital workflows? How do you manage resources effectively? I'll provide practical advice for working with departments like finance, human resources, and operations to ensure that you have the support you need to succeed.

Of course, one of the most important aspects of your job is managing people. Your team is your most valuable asset, and leading them effectively is key to your success. We'll cover strategies for building strong relationships, fostering a collaborative culture, and handling conflicts that inevitably arise in a fast-paced healthcare environment.

Finally, we'll talk about how to stay agile in a constantly changing healthcare landscape. Whether it's adapting to new regulations, implementing the latest technology, or meeting evolving patient needs, being a service line leader means staying ahead of the curve. I'll share insights on how to remain flexible and forward-thinking, so you can continue leading your team and your service line successfully.

A Journey of Growth

One of the most important things I want you to take away from this book is that leadership is a journey. No one expects you to have all the answers right away, and that's okay. What matters is your commitment to continuous growth and improvement. Be open to feedback, stay curious, and never stop learning.

The challenges you'll face are opportunities to grow as a leader. Whether you're navigating a staffing shortage, implementing a new electronic health record system, or managing a departmental budget shortfall, each obstacle you overcome will make you a stronger, more resilient leader.

This book is designed to be a resource for you on that journey. It's not a one-time read but a guide you can return to as you face new challenges or need fresh perspective. Whether you're just starting out or you've been in the role for a while, I hope you'll find useful insights and strategies that resonate with you and help you lead with confidence.

Service line leadership is an incredibly rewarding role, but it's not without its challenges. This book will help you build the foundation you need to excel in your new role, offering practical guidance on everything from developing a strategic vision to managing a multidisciplinary team. Along the way, you'll learn how to balance clinical excellence with financial sustainability and how to create an environment where both your team and your patients can thrive.

So, let's get started. You're about to embark on an exciting journey as a service line leader, and I'm here to guide you every step of the way. Welcome to leadership—you've got this!

Chapter 1: The Role of a Service Line Leader

Welcome to the role of service line leader, where your responsibilities go far beyond managing day-to-day operations. This position places you in a unique space—at the intersection of clinical excellence, operational efficiency, and financial sustainability. You're not just overseeing tasks; you're creating an environment where patient care thrives, where the organization's financial goals are met, and where sustainable growth becomes the norm. You are the bridge between the hands-on work your team performs and the larger vision your organization aims to achieve. This role is challenging, but with the right foundation, you'll find it incredibly rewarding.

Leadership in healthcare isn't just about keeping things running; it's about setting the tone for your team and guiding them toward common goals. When you create a culture where collaboration, transparency, and innovation are valued, everything else—patient care, staff satisfaction, and financial success—falls into place. Your leadership influences more than just workflow or budgets; it shapes how people feel about their work and the care they provide. Your presence, your approach, and your decisions will ripple through the department, impacting both team morale and the quality of care your patients receive. In a role like this, the way you lead matters just as much as what you manage.

You might be wondering, "What exactly is a service line?" In many ways, it's like a mini-organization within the larger hospital or health system. Whether you're leading neurology, oncology, or cardiology, the idea is the same—each service line is focused on delivering specialized care for a specific patient population while optimizing resources, improving outcomes, and maintaining financial health. And as the leader of this service line, you'll have your hands in every facet, from clinical protocols to staffing decisions and financial strategy. It's a demanding role, but it's also incredibly fulfilling because you'll see firsthand the impact of your leadership on both your team and the patients you serve.

This book is here to guide you through the complexities of service line leadership. It's designed to help you blend your clinical knowledge and operational expertise with leadership skills in a way that elevates your department. Whether you're stepping into this role from a clinical or administrative background, the challenges you'll face require more than just what you've learned in school or through experience—it takes a mix of practical strategies and real-world insights to truly thrive. That's what this book is all about—giving you the tools to not just survive in this role, but to excel.

One of the first pillars of becoming an effective service line leader is clinical expertise. If you've spent years working in clinical settings, you already have a head start. But if you're coming from more of an administrative or operational background, now is the time to roll up your sleeves and immerse yourself in the clinical side. Spend time shadowing your team, observing procedures, and understanding the day-to-day realities of patient care. This isn't just about learning the technical details—it's about building trust with your team. When they see you actively engaging with the clinical aspects of the service line, they'll know that you're invested in their work. And if you're already experienced in clinical care, the key is to stay up-to-date. Healthcare is constantly evolving, and as a leader, it's your job to ensure that your knowledge evolves with it. Whether that means attending conferences, engaging in continuing education, or simply staying connected with industry trends, the point is to keep growing so you can lead your team with confidence.

Of course, clinical expertise is only part of the equation. To be a well-rounded leader, you'll need to master the operational side of healthcare too. Understanding hospital operations is essential for identifying inefficiencies and driving improvements. Get involved in committees that focus on patient throughput, resource management, and workflow optimization. The more you know about how the hospital functions on a broader scale, the better equipped you'll be to make decisions that benefit your service line. For example, are there bottlenecks in patient admissions or discharges? How does your service line handle fluctuations in patient volume? By digging into these questions, you'll not only improve the efficiency of your department but also enhance the patient experience.

And then, there's the financial side. In healthcare, finances and patient care go hand in hand. While your primary focus will always be on delivering excellent care, you must also ensure that your service line is financially sustainable. This means understanding how hospital budgets work, how revenue is generated, and what drives reimbursement. Working with your finance team to interpret profit-and-loss statements and key performance indicators (KPIs) like cost-per-case or length of stay will empower you to make data-driven decisions that improve both patient outcomes and the bottom line. For instance, reducing readmission rates not only enhances care but also helps avoid financial penalties. By understanding the financial dynamics behind your service line, you can guide your department to long-term success.

Being a strong leader also requires continuous growth in leadership and management skills. Whether you choose to pursue formal education, such as a Master of Healthcare Administration, or engage in leadership development programs, the point is to never stop learning. Leadership is about more than just managing people—it's about inspiring them, resolving conflicts, and making strategic decisions that drive your department forward. Strong leaders foster a culture of collaboration, where staff feel supported and empowered to do their best work. The better you are at leading people, the better your service line will perform.

Your path to service line leadership is unique. If you come from a clinical background, use your experience to take on leadership roles within your specialty—charge nurse, clinical supervisor, or department chair are great stepping stones. These roles will allow you to learn the ropes of team management, operational decision-making, and financial oversight. If you're from an administrative background, your journey will be about getting closer to the clinical side. Build relationships with clinicians, observe patient care, and attend clinical meetings to gain the insights you need to effectively lead your team. And if you've already led a service line in another specialty, your skills in leadership, process improvement, and financial management are transferable, no matter the clinical focus.

Ultimately, becoming an exceptional service line leader requires a blend of clinical expertise, operational savvy, financial understanding, and leadership skills. By focusing on these areas, you'll be able to help your team thrive while also contributing to the success of your organization. The role is demanding, but with the right mindset and tools, you'll make a meaningful impact on both your team and the patients you serve.

Chapter 2: Building a Strategic Vision for Service Line Success

When you're stepping into service line leadership, one of the most critical tasks is developing a clear and actionable strategic vision. Think of this as your blueprint—it's what will guide your department, keep everyone focused on shared goals, and ensure that you're moving in the right direction. Without a well-defined vision, even the most well-run teams can eventually stagnate. The first step is aligning your department's objectives with the broader mission of your hospital. For example, if your hospital is focused on population health management, your service line should consider initiatives like chronic disease management or preventive care. This alignment not only positions your department for success but also helps you gain the support and resources you'll need from the larger organization.

To build an effective strategic vision, you'll need to start by assessing the current state of your service line. That means gathering both qualitative and quantitative data—look at patient outcomes, financial performance, patient satisfaction, and even your department's market share. Is there a particular area where your service line is underperforming, such as higher-than-average readmission rates or higher costs per patient?

These insights give you a baseline to work from. But data alone won't give you the full picture, so it's essential to engage key stakeholders. Physicians, nurses, administrators, and even patients can provide invaluable feedback on what's working and what needs improvement. Through focus groups, interviews, and surveys, you can uncover blind spots that data may not reveal.

Once you've done your homework, it's time to set specific, measurable, achievable, relevant, and time-bound (SMART) objectives. For example, you might aim to increase patient satisfaction scores by 10% over the next year or reduce patient falls by 15% within six months. These objectives need to align not just with your department's needs but also with the hospital's larger goals. If your organization is prioritizing the reduction of healthcare disparities, think about how your service line can contribute—whether by improving access for underserved populations or enhancing cultural competence within your team.

A strategic vision is only as good as the culture that supports it. Open communication is key here. You'll want to make sure your team fully understands the vision—not just what it is, but why it's important. Regular meetings can help keep everyone on the same page, and transparency about the steps you're taking will foster trust and engagement. Just as important is fostering a sense of ownership among your team.

When team members feel responsible for specific parts of the plan, they're more likely to be invested in its success. This is also a great way to develop leadership skills across your team. Encourage a culture of continuous improvement, making it safe for people to propose new ideas and learn from both successes and failures. This creates an environment where innovation can thrive, and your team can constantly improve.

Turning vision into action is where the real work happens. Effective delegation is key—you need to break down your strategic vision into manageable projects and ensure everyone understands their role. Give them the resources and support they need, but also hold them accountable for outcomes. Regular monitoring is equally important. Set up key performance indicators (KPIs) to track progress and have frequent check-ins with your project leaders to ensure things are on track. Be prepared to adjust your plan as needed. The healthcare landscape is always evolving, and your flexibility in adapting to these changes will be crucial to your success.

Ultimately, becoming a successful service line leader means balancing clinical expertise with strong operational and leadership skills. By laying a solid foundation, creating a strategic vision, and fostering a culture that supports it, you set the stage for both short-term successes and long-term improvements. Following this approach will put you in a strong position to lead your service line to success and make a lasting impact on patient care and the organization as a whole.

Chapter 3: Developing Collaborative Leadership

As a service line leader, your ability to foster collaboration across different teams and departments is critical to the success of your program. Healthcare is a team sport, and your role requires you to bring together professionals from diverse backgrounds and specialties, ensuring that everyone is working toward a common goal. You're not just leading your immediate team; you're connecting the dots between departments, specialists, and hospital leadership to create a cohesive system. Developing collaborative leadership isn't just about managing; it's about building relationships that enable smoother operations and better patient outcomes.

One of the first things you'll need to focus on is building an interdisciplinary team that works together seamlessly. This starts with recognizing the unique contributions of every member of your team. Whether it's physicians, nurses, physical therapists, pharmacists, or social workers, everyone has a crucial role to play in achieving your service line's objectives. Identify the key stakeholders for your initiatives, especially when the care of your patients spans multiple disciplines. For instance, if you're leading a neurosurgery service line, you'll need close collaboration with ICU nurses, physical therapists, and respiratory therapists for post-operative care.

Open communication is key here, and setting up regular meetings or daily huddles can go a long way in ensuring everyone is on the same page. These meetings should be focused and efficient, addressing patient outcomes, workflow challenges, and any concerns team members might have. Setting shared goals is another effective way to foster collaboration. When everyone sees how their specific role contributes to the larger objective, like reducing patient discharge times, they'll feel more connected to the mission.

Physician engagement is another cornerstone of successful service line leadership. Physicians are the clinical decision-makers, and without their buy-in, it's difficult to implement meaningful changes. Building trust with your physicians is essential. They need to feel confident that you understand their concerns and that any changes you propose will make their work more efficient, not more complicated. This often requires one-on-one conversations where you listen to their frustrations and invite them to share their thoughts on potential solutions. When it comes to making decisions that affect clinical operations, make sure physicians have a voice at the table. For example, if you're considering adjustments to the patient scheduling system, their input is crucial to ensure the changes work from both a clinical and operational standpoint. And remember, supporting physicians in their clinical initiatives, whether that's by securing new equipment or arranging specialized training, shows that you're committed to helping them succeed, which fosters a stronger collaborative spirit.

Collaboration doesn't stop within your department—it extends to other areas of the hospital like IT, finance, and HR. These departments play critical roles in supporting clinical care, and it's important to build strong relationships with them. Start by understanding the unique ways these departments impact your service line. For instance, IT is vital for optimizing EMR systems and other workflow tools, while HR ensures you have the right people in place to deliver care. Regular check-ins with leaders from these departments will help you stay aligned and ensure they understand your service line's priorities. When you're launching new initiatives, like a telemedicine program, engaging other departments early is essential. Work closely with IT to ensure the technology meets clinical needs and collaborate with HR to ensure staff is properly trained. Additionally, part of your role is advocating for your service line's needs—whether it's securing budget approval for new equipment from finance or negotiating with HR for more staff. You'll need to present a strong case for how these resources will enhance patient care and improve operations.

In short, leading a service line successfully means building bridges—between people, departments, and objectives. When you focus on collaborative leadership, you create an environment where every team member feels empowered to contribute, and that collective effort leads to improved patient outcomes and operational efficiency.

Chapter 4: Creating an Efficient Operational Structure

Creating an efficient operational structure is absolutely essential for the success of any service line. It's the backbone that ensures your department runs smoothly, reduces waste, and ultimately maximizes patient outcomes while keeping costs under control. As a service line leader, one of your top priorities should be to identify where your current processes may be inefficient. Whether it's the way patients move through the system, how resources are allocated, or how your staff is scheduled, you want to dig into those details to see where improvements can be made. For example, you could start by conducting a workflow analysis that maps out every step of your key processes, such as the entire journey of a patient undergoing elective surgery—from pre-op to discharge. Involving your frontline staff in this analysis is crucial because they'll give you the real, on-the-ground picture. Once you've mapped it out, look for bottlenecks. Are there unnecessary delays in the process? Are lab results or procedures taking too long to get done? Identifying these areas helps you pinpoint where the most impactful improvements can be made. Once you've done that, you can work with your team to make those changes, possibly using lean management principles or Six Sigma techniques to fine-tune your operations.

Optimizing how you manage your resources is another key part of building an efficient service line. Staff, equipment, and supplies are the pillars that keep everything running, but they have to be managed carefully to ensure both quality care and cost-efficiency. Start by taking a deep dive into what you're currently working with—conduct a resource inventory. Are you scheduling your operating rooms effectively? Are there underutilized machines or spaces? Once you've gathered that information, you can align those resources more closely with patient demand. For example, if your operating room schedules are always tight, you might look into extending hours or adding staff during peak times to accommodate both elective and emergency cases. Staffing, in particular, is one of the largest expenses in healthcare, so you want to make sure your workforce is being used efficiently. Adjusting shifts to match patient volumes or cross-training staff so they can float between different areas, like pre-op and post-op, can make a huge difference in how well your team operates.

Technology plays a huge role in driving operational efficiency as well. From automating routine administrative tasks to improving patient care through data-driven decisions, tech can be your greatest asset. One place to start is by adopting workflow automation tools—these can help take care of repetitive tasks like appointment scheduling or surgical inventory tracking, freeing up your staff to focus more on direct patient care. Another powerful tool at your disposal is data analytics.

By working closely with your IT department, you can set up dashboards that track everything from patient outcomes to operational efficiency and financial performance. This data allows you to make informed, data-driven decisions and measure the success of your initiatives. Additionally, if your hospital uses electronic medical records (EMRs), make sure your service line is fully integrated. A well-implemented EMR system not only improves communication between departments but also reduces errors and enhances the patient experience. Collaborate with IT to ensure the EMR system is customized to meet the specific needs of your service line, making everything from patient care to resource management more streamlined and efficient.

In sum, building an efficient operational structure involves looking at your processes, resources, and technology with a critical eye. It's about continuously finding ways to improve, streamline, and optimize—all with the goal of delivering better patient care in a more cost-effective and sustainable way.

Chapter 5: Enhancing Patient Experience

Enhancing the patient experience is one of the most important aspects of service line leadership. It's not just about clinical outcomes but also about how patients feel throughout their care journey. A positive experience can improve satisfaction scores, but more importantly, it can directly impact patient recovery and long-term health outcomes. As a leader, your goal is to make sure that your department delivers compassionate, patient-centered care at every touchpoint. One of the most effective ways to do this is by prioritizing communication with patients and their families. When communication is clear, patients feel more comfortable, and they are better equipped to follow through on their care plans. Make sure your team is trained on communication best practices, whether that's explaining complex medical information in layman's terms or actively listening to patient concerns. Simple gestures, like nurses explaining post-surgery expectations, can significantly reduce patient anxiety. It's also important to involve families in the care process when appropriate. Family members can be an invaluable support system for the patient and play a critical role in care adherence after discharge. And of course, patient feedback is gold. Actively seek it out and use it to drive improvements. If you consistently hear that patients are frustrated with long wait times, for example, you can address that by improving your scheduling processes or better communicating expected delays.

Speaking of wait times, they're one of the most common complaints you'll hear as a service line leader, and for good reason. Long waits can be frustrating, and they can significantly impact patient satisfaction. Reducing those wait times should be a priority. Start by collecting data to really understand where the delays are happening—whether it's at the initial scheduling stage, in the clinic, or for a procedure like surgery. Once you have that data, look at how you can improve scheduling. Maybe that means staggering appointments differently, offering telemedicine for follow-ups, or using predictive analytics to better anticipate patient flow. Beyond scheduling, internal workflows can also be optimized. In a surgical service line, for instance, you might examine the preoperative process to make sure everything from lab results to patient prep is happening efficiently. Standardizing protocols, like using pre-surgical checklists, can help eliminate unnecessary delays. Don't forget the importance of setting realistic expectations with patients. Sometimes delays are unavoidable, but clear communication can prevent frustration. Consider using dashboards in waiting rooms or patient portals to keep patients informed about their expected wait times or the status of their procedure.

Continuity of care is another essential component of a positive patient experience. Patients need to feel that their care is seamless, from the moment they enter your service line until they are discharged or transitioned to another level of care. One way to ensure this is by developing clear handoff protocols between teams or departments. In neurosurgery, for instance, the handoff between the surgical team and the ICU is critical for patient safety and the overall success of the treatment plan.

A smooth handoff ensures that no important information falls through the cracks. For more complex cases, a multidisciplinary care plan should be developed early, with input from all relevant teams—physicians, nurses, therapists, and social workers—so that the care plan is truly holistic and patient-centered. Finally, remember that the patient experience doesn't end at discharge. Post-discharge follow-up is essential to make sure patients are recovering well at home. Whether it's through follow-up calls, telemedicine check-ins, or coordination with outpatient providers, these efforts will ensure continuity of care and help maintain high levels of patient satisfaction even after they've left your service.

Chapter 6: Managing Financial Performance

Managing financial performance is one of the most crucial responsibilities you'll take on as a service line leader. It's not just about keeping your department afloat but about finding that sweet spot where you're delivering high-quality care while also controlling costs and maximizing revenue. Balancing these elements will ensure the sustainability and growth of your service line, and it all starts with strong financial management.

One of the first things you'll need to get a handle on is your budget. Budget management is at the core of your department's financial health, and it's critical to work closely with your finance team to develop a detailed budget plan. This plan should reflect everything your department needs to run smoothly, from staffing and equipment to supplies and any capital expenditures you anticipate. It's also a good idea to build in some contingency funds. You never know when you might need emergency repairs or when patient volume will spike unexpectedly, so having a cushion in your budget can save you a lot of headaches down the line.

Once your budget is set, you'll want to stay on top of it by regularly reviewing financial reports. This will help you catch any overspending or anomalies early. For instance, if you notice that your supply costs are creeping up faster than anticipated, it's time to dig in and figure out why. Is it due to price increases, or is there inefficiency in how supplies are being ordered? Monitoring expenses regularly will give you a clear view of where adjustments are needed.

Speaking of adjustments, cost-containment strategies are your best friend when trying to keep spending in check without cutting corners on patient care. This might mean negotiating better deals with suppliers, finding ways to reduce waste, or even cross-training your staff to be more versatile. For example, in a neurosurgical unit, you might look into how surgical tools are being maintained and used to ensure that expensive equipment isn't being wasted. Small changes can add up to big savings.

While managing costs is crucial, it's only half the equation. You'll also need to focus on generating revenue for your service line. One of the key areas to start with is optimizing your billing and coding practices. This might not be the most glamorous part of the job, but it's essential. If there are mistakes in how services are billed, you could be losing out on significant revenue or facing denied claims. Work with your billing team to ensure that everything is being coded and billed accurately. Regular training sessions for your clinical staff can help them understand the importance of proper documentation, which directly impacts reimbursement.

Another way to boost revenue is by expanding the services you offer. Think about what's in demand in your region and how your department can meet those needs. For example, if you're leading a neurosurgery service line, you could consider adding specialized programs, like an epilepsy or spinal care center. Conducting a market analysis can help you identify services that align with your team's expertise and have the potential to attract more patients.

Building a strong referral network is also a key strategy for generating revenue. The more referrals you have coming into your service line, the more patients you'll be able to serve. Developing strong relationships with referring physicians and other healthcare providers in your area is essential for this. Consider hosting educational events, attending local medical conferences, or setting up regular meetings with potential referral sources. This gives you the chance to showcase your team's capabilities and expertise, and it keeps your service line top of mind when they're thinking about where to send their patients.

Ultimately, financial management in a healthcare setting is about being proactive and strategic. It's about looking for opportunities to reduce costs without sacrificing quality and finding ways to grow revenue through smart service offerings and strong referral relationships. With a solid financial plan in place, you'll be well-positioned to lead a thriving service line that delivers great care and meets its financial goals.

Chapter 7: Fostering Innovation and Continuous Improvement

In today's ever-evolving healthcare landscape, fostering a culture of innovation and continuous improvement is crucial for any service line leader. It's about more than just keeping up with the latest trends—it's about driving meaningful change that enhances patient care, streamlines operations, and keeps your department competitive. Let's dive into how you can create that kind of environment within your team.

Encouraging innovation is key to making progress. As a leader, you want to build an atmosphere where fresh ideas can flourish. One effective way to do this is by forming innovation teams. These small, interdisciplinary groups should be dedicated to identifying opportunities for improvement or exploring new approaches to patient care. Let them meet regularly and give them a clear path for submitting and testing their ideas. This keeps the creative juices flowing and provides a structured way to explore new possibilities.

Another part of staying innovative is being open to piloting new technologies. Keep an eye on emerging tools or techniques that could benefit your service line, whether it's cutting-edge imaging technology or minimally invasive surgical methods in neurosurgery. The key is to evaluate new technologies carefully and implement them in a way that's both controlled and cost-effective. Work with your team to figure out what's worth trying and how you can introduce it without overwhelming your resources.

It's important to also cultivate a "fail-fast" mentality within your department. Innovation inherently comes with risks, and not every idea will work out. Encourage your team to experiment without fear, knowing that it's okay if something doesn't pan out right away. By testing new approaches quickly and being ready to pivot if something doesn't work, you'll create a culture where people feel empowered to take risks, learn from them, and try again.

Alongside innovation, you also need to keep your department focused on continuous improvement. This is about making incremental changes that add up to significant progress over time. A good way to start is by implementing a structured continuous improvement process. Whether it's through Lean, Six Sigma, or another methodology, having a clear framework for identifying problem areas, testing solutions, and measuring success is key. And don't forget to involve everyone in this process—each team member should feel empowered to suggest changes.

Tracking your performance metrics is another critical piece of the puzzle. You'll want to regularly review data like patient satisfaction, surgical outcomes, readmission rates, or even staff productivity. Setting up an easy-to-read dashboard can help you keep an eye on these metrics at a glance, making it easier to spot where improvements are needed and track progress over time.

Finally, don't underestimate the power of celebrating small wins. Continuous improvement can feel like a long haul, so take the time to recognize when progress is made, even if it's just small steps. Whether it's a reduction in patient wait times, better discharge planning, or improved team morale, acknowledging these achievements keeps everyone motivated and reminds your team that they're moving in the right direction.

By fostering both innovation and continuous improvement, you'll create a dynamic service line that not only adapts to changes in healthcare but leads the way in delivering top-notch patient care and operational excellence.

Chapter 8: Navigating Regulatory and Compliance Challenges

Navigating the complex world of healthcare regulations is a critical part of your role as a service line leader. Compliance isn't just about avoiding penalties—it's about ensuring patient safety, maintaining quality care, and protecting your department's reputation. Let's break down how you can stay on top of regulatory and compliance challenges while leading your team effectively.

First, it's crucial to have a deep understanding of the regulatory landscape that governs healthcare. This includes both federal and state regulations, as well as your hospital's specific policies. Healthcare regulations are constantly evolving, and staying informed is essential. One way to do this is by subscribing to relevant healthcare newsletters, attending regulatory webinars, or working closely with your hospital's compliance department. You don't have to be a regulatory expert, but you do need to be in the loop on changes that could impact your service line.

Once you're up to speed, it's equally important to ensure your team understands the significance of regulatory compliance. Everyone needs to be aware of the rules that apply to their specific roles. Regular training sessions or updates in team meetings can help reinforce this. For example, in neurosurgery, keeping your team informed on protocols for sterilization and proper documentation is crucial. Not only does it protect your patients, but it also helps avoid costly penalties and ensures your department operates smoothly.

One of the best ways to maintain compliance is by having a solid audit system in place. Collaborate with your hospital's compliance department to develop a routine process that checks whether your service line is adhering to the necessary regulations. This could include spot checks on patient records, infection control practices, or even billing procedures. Regular audits ensure you catch any issues early and provide peace of mind that your department is operating within the required guidelines.

By staying informed, educating your team, and regularly auditing your processes, you'll keep your department on the right side of regulations and focus on what truly matters: delivering high-quality, safe, and compliant patient care.

Chapter 9: Leading Through Change

Leading through change is one of the biggest challenges you'll face as a service line leader, but it's also one of the most important. Healthcare is constantly evolving—whether it's adopting new technology, responding to organizational shifts, or navigating external forces like policy changes or pandemics. Your role is to guide your team through these transitions effectively, making sure they're prepared, supported, and engaged along the way.

First and foremost, communication is key. As soon as you're aware of a change, start talking about it with your team. Being transparent about what's coming, why it's happening, and how it will impact them helps to alleviate anxiety and build trust. For instance, if you're rolling out a new EMR system, explain the reasons behind the switch and highlight the benefits early on. Make sure to address any concerns upfront, so your team feels informed and involved from the start.

Another essential step is making sure your team is equipped with the right tools to handle the change. Most transitions come with a learning curve, so providing adequate training and resources is crucial. Whether it's hands-on sessions, online tutorials, or even just a support hotline they can call during the transition, giving your team the knowledge they need will set them up for success.

One thing to remember: you don't have to do this alone. Involving key stakeholders early on can make a world of difference. Whether it's working with IT, finance, or other departments like outpatient services, getting everyone on the same page early helps to ensure a smooth transition. For example, if you're implementing a new surgical protocol, bring in teams like anesthesia and nursing during the planning phase so they can offer input and help identify potential roadblocks.

As the change unfolds, make it a point to check in with your team regularly. Encourage open communication, so they feel comfortable sharing their feedback. If something isn't working, be ready to make adjustments. Change rarely goes perfectly the first time around, but being flexible and responsive can make all the difference in how your team experiences the process.

Now, resistance to change is inevitable. People get comfortable with the way things are, and even necessary changes can feel unsettling. The key to managing resistance is to address it head-on. Meet with those who are struggling, listen to their concerns, and talk them through the reasons behind the change. For instance, if your staff is unsure about a new documentation system, walk them through how it will improve patient care and lighten their administrative load.

One of the most effective ways to ease resistance is by highlighting the benefits. Show your team how the change will not only improve outcomes for patients but also make their work easier or more fulfilling. Maybe it's streamlining their workflow or enhancing work-life balance—whatever the case, framing the change in a positive light can help shift their perspective.

Lastly, don't forget to offer ongoing support. Change can be stressful, and your team will need reassurance and guidance throughout the transition. Whether it's additional staffing to ease the burden during implementation, technical support, or one-on-one coaching, make sure you're there to help them navigate any bumps in the road. And remind them that asking for help is encouraged—it's all part of the process.

With the right approach, leading through change becomes less about managing disruption and more about empowering your team to adapt, grow, and ultimately succeed in a constantly evolving healthcare environment.

Chapter 10: Developing and Retaining Talent

Developing and retaining talent is one of the most critical responsibilities you'll have as a service line leader. The success of your department doesn't just depend on you—it depends on the skills, dedication, and engagement of your entire team. So, how do you ensure your staff continues to grow and stick around for the long haul? Let's dive into some practical strategies that will help you develop your team and keep them invested.

First, let's talk about talent development. Every member of your team has their own career goals, and it's your job to help them get there. A great starting point is to create individual development plans for each person. Sit down with your staff and figure out where they want to go in their careers and what skills they need to develop to get there. Maybe you have a physician assistant who wants to specialize in epilepsy care, or a nurse who's aiming for a leadership role. Work with them to identify the right training opportunities, mentorship, or certifications that can help them reach those goals.

Another important piece of this puzzle is feedback—consistent, constructive, and timely. Don't wait for the annual performance review to talk about how your team is doing. If someone handles a difficult patient case exceptionally well, let them know right then and there. And if there's room for improvement, address it early so they can correct course. Feedback, both positive and developmental, helps your team feel seen, appreciated, and motivated to keep improving.

Continuing education is another big factor. In healthcare, staying on top of the latest techniques, treatments, and technology is a must. Encourage your team to take advantage of continuing education opportunities, whether that's attending a conference, signing up for online courses, or joining a hospital-led training program. Especially in specialties like neurosurgery, where advancements are constant, it's critical that your team stays ahead of the curve. Make sure they have access to the resources they need to grow.

Now, even if you're doing everything right in terms of development, retaining top talent is just as crucial—and it's not always easy. High turnover can disrupt patient care and cost your department time and money, so it's vital to keep your team engaged and satisfied. One of the most effective ways to retain staff is by fostering a positive work environment. This means encouraging a culture of respect, collaboration, and open communication. Address conflicts quickly and fairly, and make sure your team knows they're supported. Simple things like team-building activities or peer recognition can go a long way in keeping morale high.

Recognition is key, too. People want to feel appreciated for their hard work. Whether it's a quick "thank you" for going the extra mile or a formal employee recognition program, showing your team that you value their contributions can make a significant impact. Neurosurgery, for example, is a high-pressure environment, and a little appreciation can go a long way in preventing burnout and boosting retention.

Career advancement opportunities are another big reason why people either stay or leave. If your top performers don't see a clear path for growth within your service line, they may start looking elsewhere. Make sure you're promoting from within when possible, offering leadership development programs, or giving staff the chance to take on more responsibility in areas that interest them. When people feel like they're advancing in their careers, they're much more likely to stay.

Finally, competitive compensation and benefits matter. While salary alone won't keep someone in a job they don't like, it's definitely a factor. Ensure that your team is being paid fairly according to market standards, and think about offering additional perks. Flexible scheduling, wellness programs, or tuition reimbursement for advanced education can be particularly attractive to healthcare professionals who are balancing demanding jobs with their personal lives.

By focusing on developing and retaining talent, alongside other key leadership areas like financial management, innovation, and patient experience, you'll set your service line up for success. Your team will feel supported, motivated, and ready to deliver the best possible care to your patients—and that's the ultimate goal.

Chapter 11: Ethical Leadership in Healthcare

Welcome to one of the most crucial aspects of your new role—ethical leadership. As a service line leader, you'll be faced with difficult choices that require more than just clinical or operational know-how. Navigating the ethical landscape of healthcare is about ensuring that your decisions are not only effective but also morally sound. Let's talk about what that looks like in practice.

In healthcare, you're going to encounter ethical dilemmas all the time. Whether it's about making tough calls regarding patient care, figuring out how to allocate limited resources, or balancing financial pressures with quality of care, there's rarely a clear right or wrong answer. A good starting point is recognizing that these situations are complex. Rather than searching for a perfect solution, focus on developing a thoughtful, consistent approach.

One of the most effective ways to handle these dilemmas is by creating an environment where your team feels comfortable discussing ethical concerns. For example, if you're faced with a decision about how to prioritize care when resources are tight, don't make that call in isolation. Bring your team into the conversation. Talk about principles like fairness and equity, and explore the potential impact of different options on both patient care and team morale. When you engage your team, you're not just making better-informed decisions—you're also building a culture of trust and respect where everyone feels heard.

At the core of ethical leadership is patient-centered decision-making. This means putting the patient's best interest front and center, even when it complicates things. It's not just about following protocols; it's about understanding the patient's values and preferences. Take the time to really get to know each patient's unique circumstances. For instance, if a patient is unsure about a proposed treatment, don't rush them into a decision. Sit down with them, discuss their concerns, and make sure they understand all of their options—both the benefits and the risks. By involving them in the decision-making process, you're reinforcing their trust in your team and ensuring they feel respected and understood.

Transparency and integrity are cornerstones of ethical leadership. It's vital that your team—and your patients—feel confident that you're always operating with honesty and openness. If something goes wrong, don't brush it under the rug. Own the mistake, talk about what happened, and focus on how you can prevent it from happening again. These moments, while tough, are opportunities for growth. And when it comes to the bigger picture, make sure you're regularly communicating about the goals and challenges your department faces. Being upfront about how decisions are made and why certain actions are taken strengthens trust across your team.

Creating an inclusive and equitable work environment is also a key part of ethical leadership. Your role as a leader involves making sure everyone on your team feels valued and supported, regardless of their background. That means promoting diversity in your hiring practices and ensuring all staff have access to the resources they need to succeed. Go beyond simply checking boxes—actively encourage diverse perspectives, especially when decisions are being made. When you implement new policies or changes, gather input from a variety of voices. By ensuring that everyone has a seat at the table, you're not only fostering a more engaged team but also setting an example of fairness and inclusion.

In the end, ethical leadership is about making decisions that are not just clinically or operationally sound but also morally right. By thoughtfully navigating ethical challenges, prioritizing patient-centered care, promoting a culture of transparency, and fostering inclusivity, you'll build a strong foundation for your success as a service line leader. And in doing so, you'll inspire the same values in those around you.

Conclusion

We've covered a lot, haven't we? Service line leadership is a journey that involves balancing big-picture vision with the everyday realities of managing a team, caring for patients, and hitting organizational goals. At the heart of it all is learning how to blend long-term planning with the day-to-day operations that keep everything running smoothly. It's about setting a strong strategic foundation that aligns your service line with the broader goals of your healthcare organization. That way, when the market shifts or patient needs evolve, you're ready to adapt and thrive—not just react.

But none of this happens in isolation. Building a high-performing team is key to turning your vision into reality. Your success depends on creating a motivated, skilled, and collaborative workforce. By investing in professional development and encouraging teamwork across different functions, you'll empower your team to work together toward shared objectives. And don't forget—this collaboration extends to patient care too. Improving the patient journey and building trust within your community should always be top of mind. Focusing on the patient experience doesn't just meet expectations—it helps exceed them, creating long-term loyalty and satisfaction.

Of course, none of this works without good management. Staying proactive about operational efficiency, marketing, and risk management is critical. Streamlining workflows, managing resources wisely, and controlling costs are all essential parts of the job. And while you're making sure your operations run smoothly, don't overlook the importance of building a strong brand and communicating effectively with your patients and the broader community. Embracing new technologies and innovations can also give you an edge, helping to improve clinical outcomes and set your service line apart from the competition. Finally, never lose sight of regulatory compliance and risk management—patient safety is your top priority, and staying vigilant here will ensure your service line remains strong in the face of challenges.

In short, being a successful service line leader is about balancing many moving parts—strategic planning, operational efficiency, patient care, team collaboration, and financial responsibility. If you take the insights and strategies we've talked about throughout this book and apply them thoughtfully, you'll be well-equipped to build a high-performing service line that not only delivers outstanding care but also fosters strong relationships with both your physicians and patients. You'll be setting yourself up for long-term success in a constantly changing healthcare landscape. Yes, the road to success requires adaptability, vision, and a commitment to continuous improvement, but with the right strategies, you can make a real and lasting impact on both your team and your organization.

www.ingramcontent.com/pod-product-compliance
Lightning Source LLC
Chambersburg PA
CBHW030057230526
45471CB00003B/1135